MW01064913

The
Buffalo
Train Ride

The Buffalo Train Ride

by
Desiree Morrison Webber

Line Illustrations by
Sandy Shropshire

EAKIN PRESS ✺ Austin, Texas

Many thanks to
Molly Levite Griffis and
Darleen Bailey Beard

Author's Note

The great shaggy beasts we call buffalo are really bison. (The scientific classification for the plains bison is *Bison bison bison*.) Historically, though, Americans have called their bison "buffalo." So, that is the custom I follow in this story.

Acknowledgments

My thanks to the following individuals and institutions for their valuable assistance: Claudine Daniels—Wichita Mountains Wildlife Refuge; Towana Spivey—Fort Sill Museum; Deborah Baroff—Museum of the Great Plains; Steven P. Johnson, Library, and Dian Shapiro, Media Services—Wildlife Conservation Society (previously the New York Zoological Society); Lee Goode—J. M. Davis Arms & Historical Museum; Louise James—Plains Indians & Pioneers Museum; Roger Harris, Bob Rea, and others—Oklahoma Historical Society; Billy Evans Horse—Chairman of the Oklahoma Kiowa Tribe; Kansas State Historical Society; Panhandle-Plains Historical Museum Research Center; Eldon Clemence (Garden City, Kansas); Jack Haley (Roosevelt, Oklahoma); Pete Scholls, National Archives and Records Administration—Southwest Region; Edwin Drummond—Wichita Mountains Wildlife Refuge; Railroad Museum of Oklahoma; Melecia Caruthers and Annette Coppenbarger, Interlibrary Loan, Oklahoma Department of Libraries.

Special thanks to Donna Norvell, who told me the story.

Table of Contents

Prologue

Oil lamps swung in rhythm to the train. Elwin Sanborn heard the click-clack of the tracks beneath the train as he sped toward Buffalo, New York. The walls of the livestock car were thin—nothing more than a small barn upon steel wheels.

Sanborn lay down on his bed of hay. The sweet, grassy smell filled the air. Next to him sat a large, wooden crate. He could hear heavy expulsions of breath, a snort, and movement inside. Suddenly through the slats emerged a long, narrow tongue. It wrapped itself around a thatch of hay and jerked. Sanborn sat up with a start. He wondered if his bed would last through the night.

Ahead of him, toward the opposite end of the car, stood six crates and one metal cage. Each contained a buffalo. On top of two of the crates slept Frank Rush from the Oklahoma Territory. He reclined on blankets as if sleeping on the open range. Stretched out next to Sanborn lay Mitchell, a co-worker from the New York Zoological Park.

Sanborn lay back down again. There was no other place to bunk. His ill-mannered roommate could have all the hay he desired. No one wanted trouble. Only a wooden box separated him from a powerful set of horns. Each crate was built to carry a buffalo's weight, but would it contain an angry bison bent on fury? Tonight, and the next, and the next, he would sleep on the floor alongside this bed-robbing buffalo.

But what an adventure! They were traveling from New York to Oklahoma Territory to save the buffalo from extinction . . . if all things happened as planned.

CHAPTER 1

Masters of the Plains

Buffalo were the super-discount markets of the plains. They provided food, shelter, clothing, and weapons for the Plains Indians.

Tanned hides fashioned teepee covers, dresses, shirts, and even diapers. Dried buffalo dung was pounded into baby powder or used as fuel on the tree-less landscape. Rib bones lashed together made a sled. Clavicle bones carried written messages. Glue, from boiled hooves, fastened feathers to arrows. Tongues made a tasty treat.

Bison once ranged from Canada to northern Mexico, and from Utah east to Pennsylvania. Their true home was the Great Plains, a grassy landscape that stretched from Montana and North Dakota south to Texas. Large rivers, such as the Platte, the Missouri, and the Red, cut across its face.

Here, the bison was king.

He sniffed the endless winds for danger, ate the plentiful grasses, and drank the water which flowed from the mountains. This hairy, 2,000-pound creature was a gift from the Great Spirit. American Indians danced in the animal's honor and painted buffalo skulls on their teepees.

Many Plains Indians believed the number of buffalo to be endless. Legends told of herds swarming out of a mammoth cave beneath the earth. Each spring, the cave's mouth gaped open releasing millions of buffalo. They covered the land like a brown, velvet blanket.

Their enormous, shaggy heads held sharp horns that pointed out and upward. A thick beard hung beneath the chin. From the front, they looked wise and regal, but the rest of the body was almost comical.

Opposite the massive head was a short, thin tail ending with a tuft of hair. American Indians used the tails as fly swatters. Thick, heavy hair covered the front legs, leaving the back legs to look skinny in comparison.

Thousands of Plains Indians followed the buffalo's migration. Wherever the buffalo traveled, the tribes followed. Even though deer, elk, rabbit, and other game abounded, no other animal traveled in such large numbers. A herd provided a ready supply of meat and other useful items which kept the people fed, housed, and clothed.

Buffalo Bits

Nomadic tribes of the Southwest, including the Comanches, did not have a word for "home." (Source: Ramsay, Jack. *Sunshine on the Prairie*)

"The Herd, 1860" by M. S. Garretson.
(Courtesy Kansas State Historical Society,
Topeka, Kansas)

Looking ahead, no one would have predicted man could slaughter forty million buffalo. Looking back, it seems impossible a thousand survived.

Stories abound of the number of buffalo seen at one time. Early travelers rode past grazing herds for miles. Newspapers and magazines reported that bison herds blocked trains and steamboats for hours. Some people thought the stories were tall tales, but they were true.

Traveling down the Missouri River by steamboat in 1867, Captain Le Barge came upon a massive herd crossing the river. Buffalo poured down the riverbank, into the water, and climbed out the other side. A solid mass of bodies filled the river for four miles.

The passageway appeared blocked, but Le Barge ordered his crew to push the animals away with long poles. He succeeded in passing through, but others were not so lucky. Most of the time the steamboats were forced to wait.

George Reighard came west in 1867 and began driving a government supply wagon for General George Armstrong Custer. With others, he drove back and forth between Fort Hays, Kansas, to Fort Supply, Indian Territory (Oklahoma).

During the spring Reighard passed buffalo herds moving northward. They grazed on the new growth of grass. On one trip, traveling south toward Indian Territory, he witnessed a memorable sight.

"For 175 miles, we traveled through a continuous mass of buffalo grazing slowly northward," wrote Reighard. "In those days buffalo were not so suspicious of man as they became later, and this herd was too busy

Buffalo Bits

Jeff Durfey, an old buffalo hunter, recalled when the plains were black with bison. "I was camped once on the bank of Beaver Creek, which was six feet wide and six inches deep, with swiftly running water," said Durfey. "A buffalo herd came to the creek above our camp and drank it dry. For hours the creek bed was dry until the great herd had passed on. In 1872 [another] great herd of buffalo drank the Solomon River dry and the water in it was twenty-five feet wide and a foot deep." [Source: *Kansas City Star*, May 28, 1911]

feeding to bother us or to be frightened by us. They would lift their shaggy heads, gaze curiously at us for a moment and then go on feeding."

The enormous congregations of buffalo that Reighard, and many others, witnessed were not really one large herd. Small sub-herds moved along with other sub-herds. This gave the appearance of one large group. Some individual herds consisted of female cows and their offspring. These groups of females were led by an older cow. Mature bulls traveled in their own band except during the mating season. When spooked these small herds merged together to form a solid locomotive of thundering hooves. Running fast and hard, they were impossible to stop.

Brigadier General Dangerfield Parker, traveling to Fort Zarah, Kansas, came upon a strange sight. Looking ahead he saw a buffalo herd frozen in movement. Riding closer he found them all dead. The small herd had tried to cross a muddy stream. Blindly following the leader, they had become stuck in the mire. The hot prairie winds then dried them stiff like mummies. They stood in motion as though still alive.

Before 1870 American Indians supplied most of the buffalo robes to American and European traders. They exchanged their robes and hides for sugar, molasses, salt, beads, and other goods. The best robes came from bison hunted during the winter. In cold weather the bison's hair grew thick and woolly. Heavy with the hair, the robe kept a person warm. In summer, thick blobs of hair fell off. Then hunters killed the animal for its hide. When all the hair was scraped away, a paste made of buffalo brains was rubbed into the leather. This made it soft and pliant. The final product was sewn into clothing or teepees.

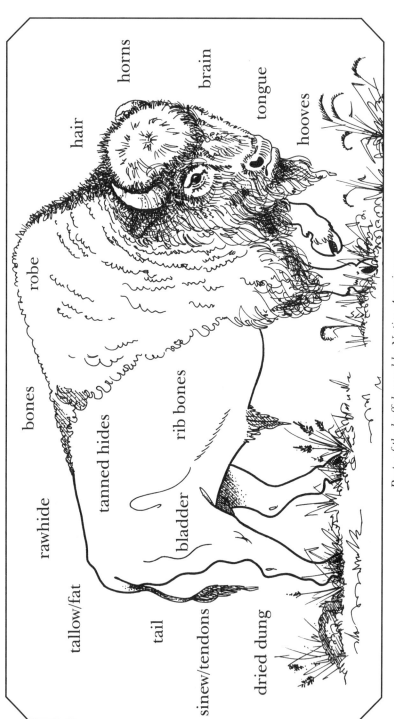

Parts of the buffalo used by Native Americans

horns

brain

tongue

hooves

hair

robe

bones

tanned hides

rib bones

rawhide

bladder

tallow/fat

tail

sinew/tendons

dried dung

The Indian method of hunting differed greatly from what the professional hunters would later develop. The Comanche and Cheyenne were, for example, skillful riders and hunters. Riding alongside a speeding buffalo, they would shoot one arrow behind the shoulder, mortally wounding the animal.

A young mountain man named Bill Hamilton met a group of Cheyenne in 1842, and they invited him on a spring buffalo hunt. At daybreak, Hamilton gathered his gun and horse. He followed fifty Cheyenne hunters as they rode out in the cold morning air. Ten miles later, scouts sighted a herd. The leader divided the men into two groups and instructed them to surround the animals. In silence, they rode a short distance from the herd. Then came the order to attack. Horses exploded to racing speed.

"There was yelling and shooting in every direction," wrote Hamilton, "and many riderless ponies were mixed in with the buffalo ... the ponies stepping into prairie-dog or badger holes. Many an Indian has come to grief by having an arm or leg broken in this way. Ponies are sure-footed, but in a run such as this one, where over a thousand buffalo are tearing at full speed over the prairie, a dust is created which makes it impossible for the ponies to see the holes...."

Hamilton continued, "All the meat required lay in an area of three quarters of a mile. I had brought down four and received great praise from the Indians. I could have done much better, but I wanted to see the Indians shoot their arrows, which many of them used. One arrow was sufficient to bring the buffalo to its knees. They shot behind the shoulder, sending the arrow deep enough to strike the lungs."

Some tribes, including the Assiniboine, Blackfoot,

and Gros Ventre, had a hunting method that killed hundreds of buffalo at one time. They chased the buffalo into traps made of trees and logs lashed together. The buffalo ran into these circular pens in a wild frenzy. Their massive bodies slammed into each other with a fatal crushing force.

Another method was to stampede the animals off cliffs. At the bottom, the women waited. They removed the hides and meat that fed and clothed their families.

None of the methods used by the Indians, though, matched the lethal technique that was yet to come.

CHAPTER 2

Killing of the Buffalo

Josiah Wright Mooar was one of the first commercial buffalo hunters. When nineteen years old, he came west from Vermont. He stopped at Fort Hays, Kansas, in the fall of 1870. The young man got a job cutting wood. Buffalo were plentiful, and Mooar occasionally shot one for dinner.

That following winter he was approached by a buffalo hunter named Charles Rath. Rath worked for a fur company in Leavenworth, Kansas. He gave Mooar a contract for 500 buffalo skins at $2.25 apiece. The hides went to England, where they were processed and cut into different sizes. English factories were experimenting with leather as belts to operate machinery.

"We counted out the hides after my hunt that year to ship by local freight," said Mooar. "I found that I had fifty-seven hides in excess of my order. My brother John Mooar was a clerk in a jewelry story in New York City, and I wrote him and my brother-in-law, John

Combs, who was working there for a silk-importing firm. I was consigning fifty-seven hides to them, instructing them to watch for them, and sell them."

When the skins arrived by open wagon in downtown New York City, they caused a commotion. Not used to the smell of buffalo, horses reared wide-eyed with fright. Many bolted and tore up carts as they ran away. The uproar caught the attention of two tanners from Pennsylvania. They quickly offered John Mooar $3.50 apiece for the hides. A few weeks later the tanners returned and offered a contract for 2,000 hides at $3.50 each. John knew there was money to be made. He quit his job at the jewelry store and joined his buffalo-hunting brother out west.

The sale of those hides created a new market. Both English and American companies wanted buffalo skins for manufacturing purposes. Hundreds of hunters and skinners poured onto the prairie like syrup on pancakes.

Unlike the methods used by the Plains Indians, the commercial hunters developed a different form of hunting. It was called the "still hunt" or "stand," and it became the most destructive type of hunting. The hunter rode as close as possible to the herd without being seen or smelled. He then crawled on his knees and belly to hide behind rocks or brush. The closer he could advance, the better. Next to him, he placed two rifles and a scattering of cartridges upon the ground. As one gun became too hot from shooting, he used the other.

With the "still hunt" method, most hunters took roughly fifty buffalo a day. And there were numerous hunting outfits on the plains. Hundreds and thousands of buffalo were slaughtered each day during the 1870s and 1880s. A few, like Josiah Mooar and George Reighard, could shoot nearly one hundred bison a day.

To keep the herd from sprinting, the hunter first shot the leader. The grazing animals continued to eat grass as their companions fell to the earth beside them.

"The leader was the oldest cow in the group," said buffalo hunter George Reighard, "so the first move of the still hunter would be to drop her."

The animals near her heard the gun and looked to her. If she ran, they would run too. The wounded leader, however, just staggered and fell to the ground.

"In one and one-half hours I had fired ninety-one shots, as a count of the empty shells showed afterward, and had killed seventy-nine buffaloes. We figured that they all lay within an area of about two acres of ground," said Reighard.

"I have often heard of still hunters killing one hundred and more in one stand. On that trip I killed a few more than 3,000 buffaloes in one month, which was an average of about 100 a day."

Most hunting outfits consisted of a sharpshooter, a few skinners, and a camp cook. One person did the shooting while the skinners cleaned the buffalo and stacked the hides. Many crews stayed out for weeks, sometimes months at a time. The men became rough,

Buffalo Bits

"The buffalo's was essentially a one-track mind. . . . He was slow to learn by experience and this lack of intelligence greatly hastened the destruction of the race. The hide hunters sometimes were able to take advantage of this peculiarity to create what was known as a 'stand,' where, if not alarmed, the whole herd could be shot down while they gazed stupidly at their dying companions." [Source: *The American Bison: The Story of Its Extermination as a Wild Species and its Restoration under Federal Protection* by Martin S. Garretson, New York Zoological Society, 1938]

dirty, and smelly, especially the skinners. Grease, blood, and dirt covered their clothes. Their hair grew long and shaggy. At meal time fingers evolved into forks and spoons, and they used skinning knives to cut their meat. In rain, snow, or sunshine, they slept under the open sky.

Large freight wagons pulled by teams of horses traveled from camp to camp. They picked up the buffalo hides stacked in piles by the skinners. This arrangement allowed outfits to stay gone for long periods of time. The freight wagons then drove to railroad depots and shipped the hides back east.

During the late 1800s, railroad companies laid track across buffalo country. They looked like stitches on the big grassy belly of the plains.

The Union Pacific built westward from Omaha, Nebraska, to Cheyenne, Wyoming, between 1865 and 1867. This split the buffalo into what became known as the "southern herd" and the "northern herd." The southern herd roamed in what is now Kansas, Texas, and Oklahoma.

By chance, three separate events came together to weave destruction for the bison. First, railroads were building west across America just as the demand for hides was growing. Second, the lure of good wages

Buffalo Bits

The railroads also demanded buffalo meat for their workers. Colonel William F. Cody, known as Buffalo Bill, had a contract with the Kansas Pacific Railway in 1867. For $500 per month he delivered buffalo meat for the railroad workers. It was said he killed 4,280 buffalo in eighteen months. [Source: Hornaday, William T. *The Extermination of the American Bison*. Annual Report to the Smithsonian Institution, 1889]

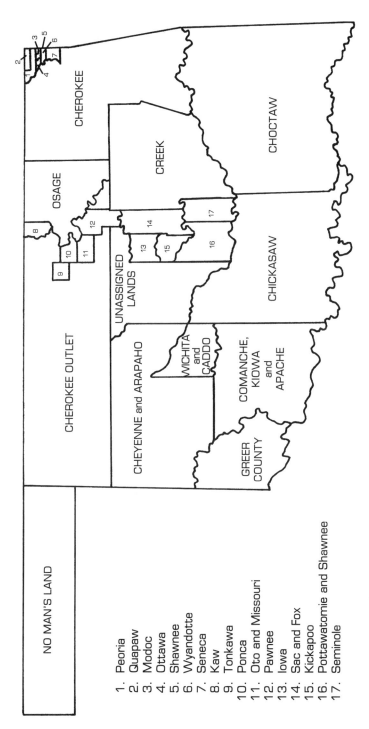

NO MAN'S LAND

CHEROKEE OUTLET

CHEROKEE

OSAGE

CREEK

CHOCTAW

UNASSIGNED LANDS

CHEYENNE and ARAPAHO

WICHITA and CADDO

CHICKASAW

COMANCHE, KIOWA and APACHE

GREER COUNTY

1. Peoria
2. Quapaw
3. Modoc
4. Ottawa
5. Shawnee
6. Wyandotte
7. Seneca
8. Kaw
9. Tonkawa
10. Ponca
11. Oto and Missouri
12. Pawnee
13. Iowa
14. Sac and Fox
15. Kickapoo
16. Pottawatomie and Shawnee
17. Seminole

INDIAN TERRITORY PRIOR TO LAND RUN OF 1889

drew buffalo hunters to the plains. With the access to railroads, hunters and hide buyers were able to ship their goods back east. Railroads transported thousands of pounds of hides, robes, and tongues by the boxcar.

The last event adding to the destruction of the buffalo was the invention of the breechloading, long-range rifle. Earlier rifles, called muzzleloaders, loaded at the top of the muzzle. Gunpowder was poured down the rifle barrel. Then the ball was added and the two had to be pressed to the bottom of the barrel with a long ramrod. After each shot, the hunter repeated the long process of reloading. With breechloading rifles, cartridges were placed easily into the chamber. The hunter reloaded and fired rapidly. The power and accuracy of these guns allowed the hunter to hide 200 to 300 yards away from the animals. The "still hunt" became possible with these guns.

Buffalo hunters descended hard upon the southern herd. Railroads continued to be built across Kansas, and this helped to ship more hides to the large cities in the east. In a few short years the southern herd was practically exterminated. Between 1871 and 1877, Kansas, Indian Territory, and Texas crawled with buffalo hunters. It was like a picnic blanket covered with hordes of unwelcome ants. Millions of buffalo were slaughtered.

Hunters killed for the money, and their actions had deadly results. Bison provided the main source of food for many American Indians. Professional hunters were destroying not only the Plains Indians' supply of food, clothing, and housing, but also how they lived. Many tribes, such as the Comanche, Kiowa, and Crow, did not farm. Their life followed the migrating buffalo.

Such a serious threat caused a revolt. The Plains Indians began to fight for their very survival.

Several bands of Comanche declared war on the buffalo hunters invading their lands. During the slaughter of the southern herd there were many skirmishes and major battles. One of the more well-known Comanche warriors was Quanah, later known as Quanah Parker. Quanah was the son of Peta Nocona, a war chief, and Cynthia Ann Parker, a white captive who had adopted tribal life.

The Comanche had captured Cynthia Ann when she was nine years old. As a young woman she married Peta Nocona, and together they had three children including Quanah. In a battle with Texas Rangers, Cynthia Ann was taken alive and then returned, against her will, to relatives in Texas. In this same conflict, the Texas Rangers also reported they had killed Peta Nocona.

Quanah was not in that fight, but he fought his own battles against the whites. In May of 1874, Quanah's group of Quahadi Comanche, plus several members of the Kiowa, Arapaho, and Cheyenne tribes, planned to attack buffalo hunters. They targeted Adobe Walls, a supply camp for hunters in the northern panhandle of Texas.

According to the Treaty of Medicine Lodge, the buffalo hunters were not to travel south of the Kansas

Buffalo Bits

Cynthia Ann Parker tried several times to escape from her Texas relatives and return to her husband and children in the Comanche tribe. (Source: Ramsay, Jack. *Sunshine on the Prairie*)

border into Indian Territory. But herds in the Texas Panhandle lured commercial hunters across the forbidden lands. The whites were not only breaking federal laws, but also they were angering the Indians by killing their buffalo. Before the planned attack, Little Robe, a Cheyenne peace chief, warned the government to control the buffalo hunters.

"Your people make big talk and sometimes make war, if an Indian kills a white man's ox to keep his wife and children from starving," said Chief Little Robe. "What do you think my people ought to say when they see their [buffalo] killed by your race when you are not hungry?"

The army was supposed to keep buffalo hunters off the Indians' lands, but it looked the other way. The Indians did not. In the early morning hours of June 27, 1874, more than five hundred warriors attacked Adobe Walls.

Twenty-eight men and one woman fought off the assault. One of the men was Bat Masterson, who later became famous as a lawman. Masterson was a sharpshooter, as were many of the buffalo hunters. They made each bullet count.

The warriors boldly attacked. Some tried to break inside by riding to the front door and surrounding the windows. Isa-tai, a Quahadi medicine man, created a powerful protective charm against bullets for the warriors. Unknown to the others until later, one warrior accidentally killed a skunk. Isa-tai said the death of this powerful animal broke his medicine. Many Indians were wounded and killed in the battle.

Inside Adobe Walls, the buffalo hunters and merchants holed up with few losses. When at last the warriors pulled back, the survivors swiftly abandoned the supply camp. The incident sparked a year-long war. Comanche and other tribes attacked soldiers, Texas Rangers, ranchers, wagon trains, and others across Indian Territory, southern Kansas, Texas, and territories west of Texas.

The army was called into immediate action with orders to bring the southern Plains Indians onto reservations. The war lasted from 1874 to 1875. In the end, the United States army hounded and starved the tribes into submission.

Quanah's band were the last of the Comanche to surrender. They traveled from the Texas Panhandle to Fort Sill, Indian Territory, on June 2, 1875, and were placed on a nearby reservation. Buffalo were no longer their food source. From that time on, they depended upon the government for rations of beef.

With the Comanche and other tribes on reservations, buffalo hunters no longer felt threatened. Hunting increased on the southern plains. It continued until almost every bison was gone. As fewer hides were shipped east, prices rose. The demand for hides,

Buffalo Bits

"The buffalo is our money. It is our only resource with which to buy what we need and do not receive from the government. The robes we can prepare and trade. We love them just as the white man does his money. Just as it makes a white man feel to have his money carried away, so it makes us feel to see others killing and stealing our buffaloes, which are our cattle given to us by the Great Father above to provide us meat to eat and means to get things to wear."—Striking Eagle of the Kiowas in a letter to Indian Agent James Haworth. [Source: Haley, James L. *The Buffalo War: The History of the Red River Uprising of 1874*. Garden City, NY: Doubleday, 1976.]

Quanah Parker
(Courtesy Western History Collections, University of Oklahoma)

robes, tongues, and meat continued. So, the hunters headed north.

The Northern Pacific Railway was pushing westward into the Dakotas and Montana Territory. The tragedy of the southern herd repeated itself on the northern plains. The hunting began in 1876, but the worst years were from 1880 to 1883. The annihilation of the great northern herd ended in the winter of 1883.

Six years later, William T. Hornaday, of the United States National Museum, surveyed the number of surviving wild buffalo in the United States. The Texas Panhandle reported twenty-five. Twenty head were spotted in Colorado. Wyoming Territory had twenty-six, Montana Territory tallied ten, and the Dakotas reported four. The Northwest Territory of Canada estimated 550 wild bison.

In addition to the wild buffalo, there were captive buffalo living on private spreads. Charles Goodnight ranched in the Texas Panhandle. At the urging of his wife Mary Ann, who was concerned by the slaughter of so many bison, he began gathering the animals.

Buffalo Bits

Jim Ennis found himself alone and far from camp after surviving an attack by a buffalo bull. Ennis rolled himself in a recently skinned buffalo robe and tried to fall asleep. A cold norther blew in and froze the hide around Ennis. During the night a pack of wolves were drawn to the site by the buffalo carcass and some began tearing at the hide encasing Ennis. The episode so frightened Ennis that it turned his hair completely white. When he returned to camp the next day, his crew did not recognize him. [Source: From an interview by Josiah Wright Mooar to J. Evetts Haley, November 25, 1927]

"The End, 1883" by M. S. Garretson.
(Courtesy Kansas State Historical Society, Topeka, Kansas)

Charles Jones of Garden City, Kansas, and ranchers Charles Allard and Michel Pablo of western Montana also began collecting wild bison. In total, Hornaday reported 256 buffalo living in captivity and another 200 under federal protection in Yellowstone National Park.

By 1889 only 1,091 buffalo remained alive in North America. Less than 600 existed in the United States. Millions of magnificent animals diminished to a mere handful.

What could anyone do to bring the bison back from near extinction?

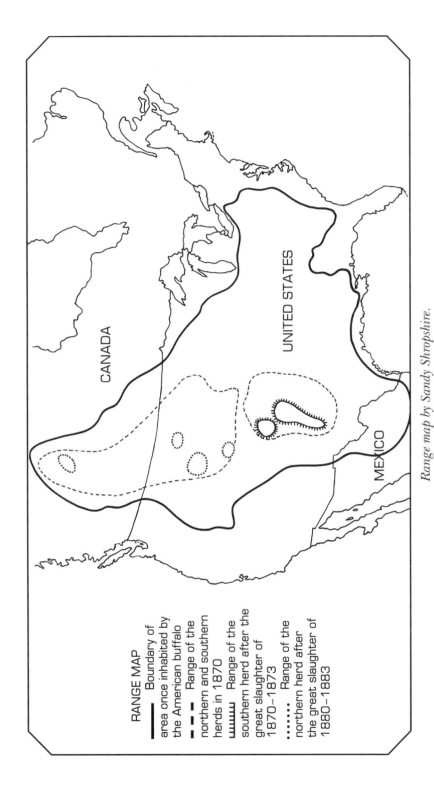

RANGE MAP

—— Boundary of
area once inhabited by
the American buffalo

--- Range of the
northern and southern
herds in 1870

⊔⊔⊔ Range of the
southern herd after the
great slaughter of
1870–1873

······ Range of the
northern herd after
the great slaughter of
1880–1883

CANADA

UNITED STATES

MEXICO

Range map by Sandy Shropshire.
(Source: "Map Illustrating the Extermination of the American Bison,"
prepared by W. T. Hornaday, 1889.)

CHAPTER 3

William T. Hornaday

The northern herd was breathing its last breath when William Hornaday became chief taxidermist for the National Museum in Washington, D.C. At that time he did not know how close the bison were to extinction. Like others, Hornaday read about the slaughter in newspapers, but the idea that millions of buffalo could be destroyed seemed impossible. Also, the event was happening 2,000 miles away—not in Hornaday's backyard where he could see it. Buffalo were being shot and skinned in a part of the United States where few people lived.

Hornaday learned of the buffalo's plight when he decided to create a bison display. He took an inventory of the museum's collection. Only two hides, plus the skeleton of a male buffalo, made up the pitiful contents. Hornaday decided the National Museum must display the continent's most important mammal. He wrote letters to army officers, ranchers, and postmasters living in buffalo country asking where he might hunt. The responses shocked him. The bison were nearly extinct.

Immediately Hornaday planned a trip to Montana. He worried the animals would be gone before he could gather specimens. There was no thought to gathering live animals, or putting a stop to the hunting. As a taxidermist, Hornaday's answer to the problem was to locate bison skins and display them in the museum. At least people would know what *Bison americanus* once looked like. In addition, the expedition would gather hides and skeletons to benefit other scientific establishments as well.

In May 1886 Hornaday arrived in Miles City, Montana, and traveled to Fort Keogh two miles away. He had arranged to work with army officers in the area. Hornaday's group asked ranchers, soldiers, hunters, and others if they had seen buffalo on the high plains of eastern Montana. People told Hornaday his search was useless. They answered all the same: "There are no buffalo anymore, and you can't get any anywhere."

Just when it looked as though Hornaday was out of luck, he received the news he needed. A rancher named Henry Phillips said a few buffalo roamed near him. Phillips owned the LU-bar ranch on the Little Dry Creek. In spite of other experts who told Hornaday there were no bison in the area, he decided to take a chance. He headed his outfit toward the isolated wasteland north of Phillips' ranch.

Phillips reported that thirty-five bison ranged in the badlands between the Little Dry and Big Dry Creeks. A thousand square miles of treeless landscape with little water stretched before them. The group spent several days looking for bison. It was like searching for thumbtacks in the desert, but Hornaday persisted. As a young man he had traveled the globe capturing cannibal fish and howler monkeys in Venezuela; flying foxes and anteaters in Borneo; tigers and elephants in India. He knew how to search long and hard for what he wanted.

At last, the expedition came upon a small herd. Instantly they chased the animals. Hornaday captured a live calf which had been unable to keep up with its mother. Ten days later they shot a bull. Tangled masses of old hair hung from its sides. The bull was shedding his winter coat. It looked rumpled and shabby; not like the specimens needed for a museum display. Hornaday desired the thick, handsome hides of winter.

He decided to take a gamble. He would go home, then return when the weather turned cold. With the onset of winter, the buffalo's pelage would be heavy with a new growth of hair. All he could do was hope the herd remained hidden in the badlands.

In late September Hornaday returned to Montana outfitted for a long hunt. With him traveled a field assistant from the University of Kansas, three cowboys, a four-man escort from Fort Keogh, a cook, food supplies, ten horses, six mules, plus 2,000 pounds of oats. The horses needed the oats to keep well fed for the rough work.

The crew did not find any buffalo until mid-October. L. S. Russell, one of the cowboys, spotted a group while he was moving camp supplies. Seven bison were tucked down in a ravine. He fired, but missed. The animals took off in a mad dash with Russell giving chase. His horse had already ridden several miles and was tired. The bison soon out-distanced the cowboy, and he was forced to give up the hunt. It was nearly dark by the time Russell returned to camp. Hornaday and his group had no choice but to wait until morning to track the bison.

At sunrise the men followed tracks into an area so dry it looked like a giant spider web. Small and large cracks laced the ground, but the earth was soft and crumbly, making it easy to see the buffalo's trail. They progressed slowly through the "gumbo ground." With each step the horses and wagon sank several inches into the powdery earth. After twelve grueling miles, the landscape changed to rolling hills of grass. The wagon rolled easier, but tracking buffalo became impossible.

At noon the group stopped to scan the hills using binoculars. Two miles away they could see their quarry resting at the top of a small butte. The herd had now doubled to fourteen. Quietly, the hunting party crept within 200 yards of the small herd. A shot was fired. The buffalo sprang to their feet and sped away with the hunters in pursuit.

"We had the most exciting and likewise dangerous chase after the herd through a vast prairie-dog town, honey-combed with holes just right for a running horse to thrust a leg in up to the knee and snap it off like a pipe-stem," wrote Hornaday.

On that day Hornaday shot a cow and a bull, and

Buffalo Bits

A full-grown male bison can run thirty-five miles per hour.

a cowhand took two bulls. One bull ran twelve miles before one of the cowboys finally overtook him. It was late afternoon by that time. So the men removed most of the meat and left the carcass for the next day.

When they returned the following morning, the buffalo robe was gone. Only the head and a scattering of broken bones remained. A group of Piegans had come during the night. They had cracked open the bones to take the marrow. The skull lay on the ground intact. They had removed only the tongue. Smeared on either side of the bull's hairy face was red and yellow paint. A thin strip of red flannel fluttered in the breeze from one horn. Hornaday was deeply disappointed by the loss, but continued with his work.

The group hunted until late November. Cold weather and heavy snowstorms forced them to stop. At the end of his trip, Hornaday had twenty-two buffalo skins plus several skeletons for mounting.

Hornaday returned to the National Museum and spent more than a year preparing and mounting the collection. When completed, a large mahogany and glass case enclosed the display. Inside stood six buffalo, including a 1,600-pound bull. All appeared gathered around a small watering hole. Hornaday's displays differed from other museums. He portrayed his animals in lifelike settings. Other museums exhibited their animals like individual statues. Hornaday used real Montana dirt and sagebrush to design a wild west scene.

While creating the display, Hornaday continually thought about the buffalo's plight. Only a small number remained alive. Why not protect and breed living buffalo? A small herd, over time, could grow into a larger herd and preserve the species. Hornaday wrote the secretary of the Smithsonian Institution and proposed a National Zoo. The plan was approved. Hornaday began in earnest to design it and build support.

He asked members of Congress for money. He drew up plans and built a model of the zoo. Everything fell into place. Seven bison, two from a private benefactor in New York and five from the Sioux reservation, were donated to the National Zoo. Besides the bison, Hornaday brought other types of animals into the collection. Crowds of people gathered each day to see the menagerie.

The National Zoo was beginning to take shape when everything came to a sudden halt. Hornaday had a new supervisor. S. P. Langley, the newly appointed secretary of the Smithsonian Institution, called Hornaday to his office.

The crowds at the zoo impressed Langley, and he decided to take charge of it. Hornaday would no longer control the project. Hornaday calmly asked for a trial period of six months to develop the zoo as he envisioned it. Langley refused. The next day Hornaday resigned and, soon afterwards, he and his wife moved to Buffalo, New York.

In his new home, Hornaday changed careers. He went into real estate and writing. He wrote two books and several magazine articles. As far as Hornaday was concerned, he was finished with zoos. Then a letter arrived from the New York Zoological Society in New York City. The Society wanted a director to start a Zoological Park.

The letter intrigued Hornaday. He could design and build a brand new zoo. There would be no question as to who was in charge. Hornaday interviewed and soon accepted the position. One of the Society's goals inspired him. It stated, "The preservation of our native animals." As the new director he could continue his interest in saving the buffalo.

Along with his wife Josephine, Hornaday planned and designed the zoological park. They took picnic lunches to a wooded area of the Bronx, a borough of New York City. Together the pair walked and planned the various enclosures. As he surveyed the grounds, Hornaday envisioned a twenty-acre range for the buffalo. The Society would build a place for the bison to live and reproduce young.

Once the New York Zoological Park was built, Hornaday contacted people who stocked buffalo on their private ranches. From Charles Goodnight, in the Texas Panhandle, he purchased three bulls and a cow. From Edward Hewins, a rancher in Indian Territory, he bought a bull, a cow, and a yearling. Other buffalo arrived a year later, and then two calves were born.

The bison herd grew in popularity with the crowds. Everyone wanted to see the masters of the Great Plains.

CHAPTER 4

A Game Preserve

Hornaday soon developed plans apart from the zoo. He pictured free roaming herds in the very areas the buffalo had once flourished. The animals would live under government protection in a place where hunting was not allowed.

Out west, however, the landscape was changing. Settlers were replacing the bison's traditional grazing lands with farms and ranches. In what became known as Oklahoma Territory, the federal government began opening acreage to homesteaders. The government divided Indian Territory in half. The western half was called Oklahoma Territory. The eastern half remained as Indian Territory with tribal nations in charge of their lands.

The first land run occurred on April 22, 1889. Settlers poured across the starting lines at noon by horse, buggy, wagon, and even bicycles to claim a section of prairie as their own. Soon others pressured the federal government to open even more tracts of land. American Indians living on reservations were forced to accept allotments. Usually every tribal member—man, woman, and child—received 160 acres, but agreements varied. Homesteaders then competed for the remaining lands.

In the southwest part of Oklahoma Territory, the Comanche, Kiowa, and Kiowa-Apache Reservation contained the beautiful Wichita Mountains. Within the Wichita's boundaries grew towering oak trees. Fresh water springs provided a haven for man, deer, coyote, wolves, and even cattle. Only thirty years earlier, herds of buffalo had grazed the broad, grassy pastures. The mountain range towered over the surrounding flat prairie land. It loomed visibly for miles from all directions.

In 1892 the U.S. government made an agreement with the Kiowa and Comanche. Each member would own 160 acres instead of possessing the entire reservation. After surveying the allotments, the United States government would open the surplus land to homesteaders. Eight years later, in June 1900, Congress approved the land for homesteading. In a short time, settlements would blanket the Reservation.

Many people did not want the Wichita Mountains divided into 160-acre homesteads. They thought the mountains should be made into a national park, like Yellowstone. The Oklahoma City Commercial Club began circulating petitions and gathered thousands of signatures. Enthusiastically, the group sent the petitions to Congress. In the spring of 1901 Congress adjourned without acting on the national park request.

Time was running out. The lands would open to homesteading before Congress met again.

Land seekers waiting in line to register for Kiowa-Comanche lottery drawing for 160-acre homesteads. "Sometimes we were compelled to stand in line for 8 hours to get our turn at the PO window." —W. R. Sharks

(Courtesy Oklahoma Historical Society, Archives and Manuscripts Division)

A few months later Oklahoma Territorial Governor William Jenkins boarded a train for Washington, D.C. President William McKinley had summoned Jenkins to help prepare the Kiowa Comanche Reservation for homesteading. Jenkins took Attorney General J.C. Strang with him. Both were strong national park supporters who refused to give up the fight. Earlier, they had discovered a law which allowed the president to set aside public lands containing timber as a national forest reserve. In addition, the president could act alone without approval by Congress. With the flourish of his pen, President McKinley could protect the Wichita Mountains from settlement.

For several days Jenkins and Strang worked with government officials. They chose a tract of 57,120 acres in the heart of the Wichitas. The forest reserve contained the high rocky summit of Mount Scott, rolling pastures, wooded hills, and clear, flowing springs. Jenkins' persistence convinced President McKinley. On July 4, 1901, the president designated the chosen acreage as the Wichita National Forest Reserve. On that very same day he also proclaimed the remaining areas open to homesteading by lottery on August 6, 1901.

With quick thinking, park promoters saved the Wichita Mountains from settlement. No one knew at the time that their actions also helped save the buffalo from extinction.

Over the next few years several people, including William Hornaday, worked toward making the Wichita Forest Reserve a game preserve. People in Oklahoma Territory, Kansas, New York, New Hampshire, and Washington, D.C., wrote letters, lectured, discussed and planned. The conservationist movement was growing in America, and it had a powerful ally.

Theodore Roosevelt became president following the assassination of William McKinley. As an outdoor enthusiast, President Roosevelt used his powers to create 125 million acres of national forest across the United States. He moved strongly on conservation and supported the idea of a game preserve to protect the bison. In January of 1905 he signed a bill that allowed him to designate the Wichita Forest Reserve as a game preserve.

Next, Hornaday asked the New York Zoological Society to offer the federal government a small number of bison to start a herd. The Society agreed to provide the animals if the government would erect a fence around the range and pay to maintain the herd. The government accepted the Society's offer. In June President Roosevelt proclaimed the entire Wichita Forest a game preserve. All animals on the Wichita National Forest and Game Preserve were now protected from hunting and trapping.

Hornaday wasted no time in designating an area to fence. In the fall of 1905 he sent J. Alden Loring to find a suitable range for the buffalo. Loring arrived by train at Cache, a small town just twelve miles south of the preserve. Immediately he took to the area by horseback. He rode the valleys, climbed the rocky hills, and viewed the landscape. Loring found buffalo wallows everywhere—evidence that the animals had once roamed the area.

In the western center of the preserve, Loring found the perfect location for a buffalo range. It contained choice grazing. Mountains, hills, and ridges surrounded the area. These high points would protect the animals from winter storms. Through the middle flowed Cache Creek. Loring stopped and drank the cold, spring-fed water.

He mapped an area roughly twelve square miles for the buffalo range. Nestled at the heart was a valley. Loring named it "Winter Valley." It would protect the herd from the harsh winter winds. Grasses grew abundantly and buffalo wallows dotted the landscape. Although the area seemed perfect for the bison range, Loring had to discover any dangers. He interviewed people living near the preserve and those who privately owned buffalo.

"During my stay in Oklahoma I interviewed many old-time plainsmen and Indians," Loring wrote in his report. Among them were Charles Goodnight, Ben Clark, Quanah Parker, and Dutch Pennah. "All of these men had hunted buffalo in the early days—some of them on the very land now being considered for buffalo range."

Loring traveled to the Texas Panhandle to talk with the famous rancher Charles Goodnight. Goodnight owned a herd of buffalo. He warned Loring that the bison could be susceptible to Texas fever—a cattle disease carried by ticks. Personally, he had never lost a buffalo to the fever, but Goodnight was an experienced cattleman. It was possible the bison would be in danger from the cattle that grazed on the preserve.

Buffalo Bits

Wallows were created by buffalo rolling their heavy bodies in the dirt to scratch their itchy skin. This rolling created circular impressions, called wallows, in the ground.

Loring also spoke with Major Gordon Lillie, owner of "Pawnee Bill's Wild West" show. Lillie, known as "Pawnee Bill," traveled all over the country with his buffalo. He knew firsthand the effects of Texas fever on the animals. Ten years earlier he had taken seven head of bison through Texas. The tour lasted six weeks, and all seven buffalo died. A veterinarian inspected Lillie's animals and pronounced the cases Texas fever. Just weeks before Loring arrived, Lillie had taken his show close to the Texas border. This time he had five buffalo with him. All five became sick, and two died. A taxidermist inspected the skins and told Lillie they were covered with ticks.

Besides Texas fever, there was another threat to buffalo—wolves. These predators were an ancient enemy of the bison. Several lived in and around the Wichita National Forest and Game Preserve. When President Roosevelt signed the law creating the preserve, the law also banned all hunting. This action protected the buffalo, but it covered every animal living on the preserve, including the wolf, as well. The preserve superintendent told Loring that wolves had killed seventy-two head of livestock in the past six months. Little doubt existed that wolves would also attack any bison placed on the preserve, especially calves.

Stories abounded of wolf packs following the buffalo herds. They searched out the sick, the weak, and the young. In one episode, witnessed by an army surgeon, a group of bulls stood in a circle with their heads facing out. A dozen hungry gray wolves paced around the group. Shielded within the knot was a newly born calf. The wolves swiveled and looped, looking for an opening to snatch dinner. The bulls lowered their horns, daring the predators to step closer.

The doctor watched as the calf would stand, walk a few feet toward the main herd, and then collapse to the ground. All the while, the bulls defended the calf from the wolves. This circle of protection lasted until the calf made it back safely to the main herd.

Predators on the Wichita National Forest and Game Preserve would have to be managed. For the small herd to establish itself, preserve officials needed to take every precaution. Loring's report, however, contained more than the dismal news of Texas fever and wolves. Loring also wrote of the people's reaction. Those living around the preserve were excited about the buffalo's return. Elder tribal members, who had once hunted buffalo, were especially pleased.

Loring spoke with Comanche leader Quanah Parker and told him that President Roosevelt was involved with the project. Parker knew Roosevelt. Earlier that year he had joined Roosevelt on a wolf hunt near Frederick, Oklahoma Territory.

"Tell the President that the buffalo is my old friend," said Parker, "and it would make my heart glad to see a herd once more roaming about Mount Scott."

Buffalo Bits

Ticks, like spiders and scorpions, are arachnids. They fasten themselves to the skin of an animal by their mouth. Using their sharp mandibles, they cut a hole in the skin and suck the blood. Through their bite, disease is passed along to an animal.

CHAPTER 5

Buffalo Are Coming!

Maybe it would work. The regal buffalo might once again appear on the southern plains of the United States. Even though he wrote of obstacles to overcome, Loring's report sparked excitement. After all, buffalo had once roamed and lived in the Wichita Mountains region. But the wolves and Texas fever ticks created thorny problems. Much work lay ahead in preparing the preserve for a bison herd.

Dealing with wolves was a lot less troublesome than dealing with ticks. Fighting a parasite posed a challenge. They had to find a way to protect the buffalo from the tick's bite.

Hornaday also worried about the buffalo wandering past the protective boundaries of the preserve. The Zoological Society asked Congress for money to fence in the twelve square miles of bison range. Lessons had been learned from losses at Yellowstone National Park. When the buffalo wandered past the park's boundaries, hunters legally shot them. Hunting laws only protected the animals while they remained inside Yellowstone.

Park rangers also had to deal with people who hunted illegally on park property. Yellowstone was so large it was hard to catch the unlawful hunters. With so few buffalo alive, prices had skyrocketed for a single head or robe. Poachers risked trouble with the law because of the money they received. A New York millionaire paid $1,500 for a single head. By 1903 poaching had taken its toll. The Yellowstone herd had dropped from two hundred bison to twenty-one head.

Hornaday did not want the same problem repeated at the Wichita National Forest and Game Preserve. The first step was to build a fence to protect the bison. Later they would hire rangers to ride the preserve and prevent any unlawful hunting. Congress passed the bill allocating money for a fence. Immediately supplies were ordered, and the project began.

Predators stood as the next problem to solve. Throughout time, wolves had played an important part in nature's ecosystem by preventing over-population. They fed on everything from mice and birds to deer,

Buffalo Bits

Bison had two natural enemies: the wolf and the grizzly bear. Wolves may have been a bison's deadliest enemy, but so was nature. A cyclone caught Mr. Ely Moore while hunting in 1854. He escaped injury but he found two unlucky buffalo. The mighty winds had completely stripped them of their hair. [Source: Garretson, Martin. *The American Bison*. New York: New York Zoological Society, 1938]

antelope, elk, and bison. Their traditional food source had been the buffalo, but now the buffalo were gone. As homesteaders settled around the Wichita Game Preserve, they brought their livestock with them. Ranchers also ran cattle on the adjoining open pastures. So wolves switched to new items on the menu: cattle and horses. This made the predators unpopular neighbors. If anyone spotted one of the four-legged creatures, they shot it. People also set traps and held organized hunts. These methods kept the numbers down, but the wolves now had a protected area.

The boundaries of the preserve provided a haven for the animals. Rocky hills, thick with brush and trees, created perfect hiding places. The "no hunting" law, written to shield the buffalo from hunters, also protected the wolves. The predators freely traveled the preserve undisturbed.

Government officials discussed the dilemma. There was no doubt the predators would attack younger members of the herd. Buffalo, as a group, were effective fighters. Caught alone an individual animal was not often victorious. Wolves would surround a lone bison, attacking it from the front and rear. The head and horns delivered mighty blows, so the wolves grabbed the rear legs, cutting the tendons. The injured animal collapsed to the ground. Unable to stand, the buffalo could no longer defend itself.

The Forest Service enacted a temporary change to its "no hunting" policy. To eradicate the wolves, large hunts and trappings took place on the preserve. In an ironic twist of fate, one species was removed to protect another.

Like others in the area, Bert Cook participated in the wolf hunts. He and his dad owned a mining claim inside the preserve near Mount Lincoln. By autumn 1906 all the wolves had been either hunted or chased off except for two nicknamed the "Mount Lincoln killers." These two had eluded hunters. Then one morning Bert Cook met one of the renowned wolves face-to-face.

"Coming around a sharp bend in the trail, I met the male wolf and I didn't need any introduction to him," said Cook. "We were about fifty or sixty feet apart. He was standing in the trail looking at me. Needless to say, I stopped too. He stood there and looked at me, wondering, I guess, what kind of animal he had met in the trail. Anyway, he leisurely turned and picked his way through the brush and rocks off to the south of the trail."

Cook was carrying a long steel drill and felt this protected him enough to follow the wolf. As he hoped, the male led him right to the den. Cook turned back to find his dad, and the two soon returned with rifles and dynamite. They were scrambling up the rocks when one of the wolves surprised them. The male raced out of his den snarling. Quickly they both shot, and the wolf went down, but they could not see the female. Bert's dad continued his climb to the den and positioned the dynamite.

"After the blast went off, I walked around a big boulder and met one of the biggest mouths I had ever seen. It was full of teeth. It wasn't over two feet from the muzzle of my gun when I pulled the trigger. Believe me, I'm still thankful that gun went off, but about all I remember was that wolf with the big mouth."

For a time this episode ended the wolf problem, but ticks were not so easy to drive away. Texas fever still presented a major obstacle. Forest Service staff and members of the Biological Survey continued to work on a solution. In addition, government officials searched for a gamekeeper. They needed someone who possessed skills and experience in handling buffalo—an individual who knew what they ate, what made them sick, and how to care for them. The gamekeeper would live on the preserve and be in charge of the herd. Everyone wanted the bison to stay healthy and strong, and produce young buffalo.

The search for an experienced handler led to Major Gordon Lillie. Lillie had acquired his own private herd of bison for his famous "Pawnee Bill's Wild West" show. Because of his business, Lillie knew other ranchers who also owned buffalo. One of them was Ed Hewins, who once owned a spread not far from Lillie's place. Frank Rush, Hewins' foreman, cared for the private herd. Lillie knew Rush. He liked and respected him. So Lillie recommended him as gamekeeper. Not only was Rush a knowledgeable handler of buffalo, but he also knew how to work with people. This would be an important asset for the preserve. The responsibilities demanded that Rush work with ranchers, farmers, miners, politicians, plus Indian tribal leaders and members.

Rush possessed a deep respect for the Indians. He was six years old when his family moved from Kentucky and settled on the wild prairies of Kansas in 1871. Their new home made a striking impression upon the young boy. Just days after arriving, Rush met an old Indian woman grieving over a terrible loss. Telling her story through sign language, she told Rush that a band of Apaches had killed her children. In her sadness, she had stabbed her feet several times with a spear.

Frank Rush, "Cowboy Naturalist"
(Courtesy Oklahoma Historical Society,
Archives and Manuscripts Division)

As a grown man Rush still held vivid memories of the woman. This first meeting was not his last. As he grew up, he encountered many nomadic tribes of Plains Indians traveling through Kansas and Indian Territory. He watched as whites pushed Indians off their lands and slaughtered the buffalo. This too made an impression on him.

When he was fifteen Rush became a cowboy. He loved the open spaces with the deer, turkey, and other wild animals. When he became foreman of Hewins' ranch, homesteaders were settling the Oklahoma Territory. Rush, himself, participated in the April 22, 1889, Land Run. He helped his sister and brother-in-law stake a claim. Over time, though, he became concerned about the destruction of wildlife, fields, and forests. He wrote letters to newspaper editors and spoke before the Territorial Legislature. He promoted hunting laws and legislation to protect native species. People nicknamed him the "cowboy naturalist."

After official interviews, the Forest Service hired Rush. Not only would he be responsible for the buffalo, but after January 1908 he would manage the Wichita National Forest and Game Preserve. Wilbur Mattoon, the current supervisor, did not want the job. He would help Rush in the beginning and then depart for another assignment within the Forest Service.

On September 3, 1907, Rush arrived at the train depot in Cache, just a few miles from the preserve. Mattoon met him at the station and helped him unload his belongings. Early the next morning Rush found himself fighting a prairie fire. The fence crew had let their cooking flame get away from them. With dry grass and prairie winds, the blaze raged out of control. All day Rush handled the water wagon. By evening the fire was contained.

Rush could see this job was going to be a lot of work. But hard work did not bother him. For more than twenty-five years, he had ridden the range through dust and heat, wind and snow. He was as tough as saddle leather. Rush had numerous ideas for the preserve, but most important was the arrival of the bison. They would survive the Texas fever and grow to be a large herd. He would see to that.

When the animals arrived they would be placed in large, fenced corrals. Roaming the range would not occur until spring. Rush wanted to eliminate the threat of Texas fever before allowing the herd to move freely.

The Texas fever tick weighed heavily on everyone's mind as it was the last remaining obstacle. If they could protect the herd from the fever, the animals had a good chance of survival. Both Rush and the Biological Survey worked hard on the tick problem.

Using a controlled fire, Forest Service employees burned the corral grounds three times. Also, when the animals arrived, they planned to spray them with crude oil. Thick hair matted in the lubricant would keep the ticks from biting the skin. Rush speculated that over time the bison would build an immunity to the fever. Then they would no longer need the crude oil.

Rush just finished preparing the corrals when orders arrived from the Forest Service. The instructions directed Rush to board the train for Washington, D.C. and then on to New York City. He was to escort the bison from the New York Zoological Park to the Wichita Game Preserve. The buffalo were coming home.

News of Rush's departure for New York City spread to Cache, Fort Sill, Lawton, and other areas near the preserve. Excitement charged the air. The Comanche and Kiowa were elated by the news of the buffalo's return. The animal had once been the center of their life. Now only buffalo wallows and dried bones dotted the plains. Their children would soon see the revered animals for themselves.

The Kiowa lived on an encampment at the base of Mount Scott. Before hearing the official news of the buffalo's arrival, a young woman had predicted their return. Months earlier Ah-Tone-Ah, daughter of Sate-Tien-Day, had been gathering wood on the north side of Mount Scott. Suddenly, the ground beneath her began to shake like an earthquake. Without warning the hillside split open, and out streamed buffalo. Dust filled the air as they thundered toward the southwest and disappeared from her sight.

Ah-Tone-Ah, unable to interpret the vision, told her family. No one thought they would ever see the buffalo again. Then news arrived from the Wichita Game Preserve. The buffalo were returning by railroad from the northeast and heading southwest, just as Ah-Tone-Ah had seen in her vision.

Rush boarded the train late Thursday evening on September 29. Most of his life had been spent on the wide, open plains. The bend of his legs showed he

Buffalo Bits

Ah-Tone-Ah means "Chasing the Enemy," and Sate-Tien-Day translates as "White Bear."

lived his life in a saddle. Now he sat on a train bound for the large, modern cities of the East.

After attending meetings in Washington, D.C., Rush arrived in New York City early Tuesday morning. He spent the entire day at the Zoological Park. Hornaday had already selected the buffalo to start the herd. He chose nine females and six males. Rush entered the buffalo enclosure and, at a respectful distance, met his fifteen traveling companions.

He gave the bulls names symbolic of their new home in Oklahoma Territory. The largest and oldest bull he called Comanche. Two younger ones he named Lone Wolf and Quanah, honoring the well-known Kiowa and Comanche chiefs who lived near the preserve. A fourth male was named Geronimo after the famous Chiricahua Apache chief. Geronimo resided as a prisoner-of-war in Fort Sill, just miles from the preserve. Rush called the youngest spike bull General Lawton after the deceased General Henry W. Lawton. Black Dog, an Osage leader, became the name for the six-month-old bull calf. The youngest female was called Lottie, and the other cows were named Black Bird, Lize, Topsy, Queen, Dolly's Mother, Snort, Lengthy, and Gypsy.

In the past, buffalo had been shipped loosely in railroad cars. Bison, however, did not behave like cattle, and this method sometimes injured the animals. Rush knew it would be difficult to herd the fifteen animals like steers. He had been a cowboy for more than twenty-five years. Domesticated cattle would eat, rest, and not leave the freight car until a cowpuncher opened the side doors with a whoop and a holler. Buffalo, no matter how tame, exhibited a stubborn streak of independence. In some shipments of buffalo,

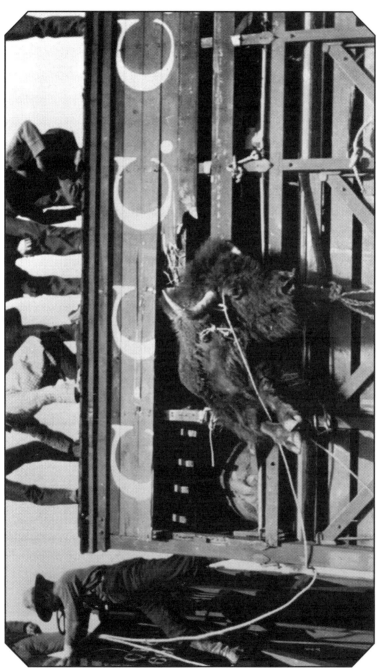

Making a last and fierce struggle for freedom.

(Photo by N. A. Forsyth,
Courtesy Montana Historical Society)

when they wanted off the train, they crashed through the wooden sidewalls of the freight car.

Rush and Hornaday decided to have individual enclosures built. Carpenters constructed solid oak crates with padding inside. Different size containers fit the dimensions of each animal. Comanche's crate stood five and half feet tall and nine feet long. Lottie's and Black Dog's containers were four feet high and only five feet long. The crates allowed the animals to eat, drink, and lie down to rest. Thick padding would protect them from the jostling and swaying of the train. The crates would also protect Rush. He could feed and water the animals without the danger of being trampled or gored.

A week after Rush arrived the loading began. The fifteen bison were separated from the rest of the herd and placed in a corral. From there, workers quickly routed each animal, one at a time, down a narrow fifty-foot chute. Lottie and Black Dog charged down the chute and through a sliding gate. As each one dashed inside the waiting crate, the door dropped shut, trapping the bison inside.

Some were not so easily directed. They hurled their bodies against the walls of the chute and refused to budge. It was like moving a bulldozer with a tooth-

Buffalo Bits

All but one buffalo had a crate built for it. For unexplained reasons, one buffalo was shipped in a wire cage. The cage, however, allowed photographers to capture an image. The reinforced, wooden crates provided little visibility. Only up close, and through the slats, could anyone have seen the bison.

William T. Hornaday (right) and Frank Rush (on top of cage) with one of the buffalo bound for Oklahoma Territory.
(Courtesy Wichita Mountains Wildlife Refuge, Indiahoma, Oklahoma)

Buffalo being loaded into crates at the New York Zoological Park.
(Courtesy Wichita Mountains Wildlife Refuge,
Indiahoma, Oklahoma)

The train cars used to ship the buffalo from New York to Oklahoma Territory.
(Courtesy Wichita Mountains Wildlife Refuge,
Indiahoma, Oklahoma)

pick. The obstinate individuals held their ground until prodded through the gate and into their padded cells.

As workers crated each bison, they slid the containers onto a wagon. Horses pulled the wagons to Fordham Station, just a short distance from the zoo. There the crates were loaded onto two waiting livestock cars. By suppertime only two more buffalo remained to be captured. A large bull and a young cow had escaped attempts to send them down the chute. The following morning the two renegades were loaded.

The New York Central, the Wells-Fargo Express Company, and the American Express Company had all agreed to transport the woolly beasts from New York City to Cache, Oklahoma Territory, at no charge. In addition, the railroad companies were connecting the livestock cars to express passenger trains. This was unusual. Such cargo normally traveled on the slower freight lines, but Hornaday selected livestock cars manufactured by the Arms Palace Horse Car Company. These cars came equipped with high and low speed air brakes and steam connections. This allowed the engineer to control the livestock cars if the train stopped for an emergency.

Early freight cars did not have such advanced equipment. Operators stopped the train by engaging the locomotive and caboose brakes at the same time. With such a crude system, freight trains traveled no faster than thirty miles per hour. Express passenger trains sped along at speeds of up to sixty miles per hour.

Hornaday wanted the bison to travel as quickly as possible. He took every precaution to protect the grand experiment. If this transfer worked, the government might be willing to locate more herds on other federal lands. A burden of responsibility rested on Rush's shoulders. Less than six hundred buffalo remained in the United States. It was not a large number to keep the species alive and thriving, but it presented a start. The Wichita Game Preserve had to be successful.

Newspapers in New York City gave little coverage of the gift to Oklahoma Territory. Animals were always coming and going from the Zoological Park. In Oklahoma Territory, though, many anxiously waited. Several Comanche had already set up camp by the buffalo yards ready to welcome their old friends home.

Late Friday night, on October 11, 1907, yardmen connected the livestock cars to New York Central's express passenger service. Frank Rush, along with two traveling companions, climbed inside livestock car 6026 with the buffalo. The three men were about to make the most memorable trip of their lives.

CHAPTER 6

Trouble on the Tracks

"All aboard!" yelled the conductor. With a jerk and an expulsion of steam, passenger train No. 37 pulled out of Fordham Station with two carloads of buffalo.

As the train reached its traveling speed, a symphony of sounds played. Against the steady thumping of the tracks, chains rattled against the walls. Stall railings banged against each other. The buffalo snorted and moaned with each sway of the train. Ceiling and wall joints creaked in the cold October air.

Frank Rush, H. Raymond Mitchell, and Elwin Sanborn climbed into one of the livestock cars. Each man gave up a comfortable passenger seat to sit nose-to-nose with a load of restless, snorting buffalo. There would be no porters with trays of hot, steaming coffee or newspapers to read; no attendant to turn down the bed sheets. Even a chair was a luxury on this trip.

Designed as miniature barns, the two livestock cars came with stalls, water tanks, and feed. One livestock car, number 6024, carried eight buffalo. In this car, the crates were placed side by side with just enough space leftover for hay and water. Rush, Mitchell, Sanborn, and the remaining seven buffalo rode together in the second car—number 6026.

Mitchell and Sanborn were employees of the New York Zoological Park. Elwin Sanborn was the zoo's staff photographer. He took along his camera equipment to capture photographs of the Wichita Game Preserve. Mitchell was Hornaday's nephew and dealt with the zoo's finances. He handled money from entrance fees and paid vendors for supplies. Mitchell knew the railroad business. The Santa Fe Railway in Oklahoma had employed him as chief clerk, cashier, and agent before he came to New York City. If any problems occurred with the train, Mitchell was to solve them.

It was 9:30, Friday night, when the group left New York City. The train hurdled through the darkness as it traveled alongside the Hudson River. The men looked out the glass windows of the doors. Reflections of light danced upon the water's surface. Reading was impossible. A few hanging oil lamps provided the only light. These swung to and fro, casting eerie shadows on the wall. With nothing else to do, the three decided to go to bed.

Bales of hay supplied the mattress stuffing. Rush took a pile and built himself a bed. Stretched out across the top of two buffalo crates, he spread a blanket and closed his eyes. Sanborn and Mitchell decided to try the floor. Each took a large amount of hay and built himself a roomy bed. Sanborn made his bunk on the side next to the bison crates.

"I can boast all my life of having slept within

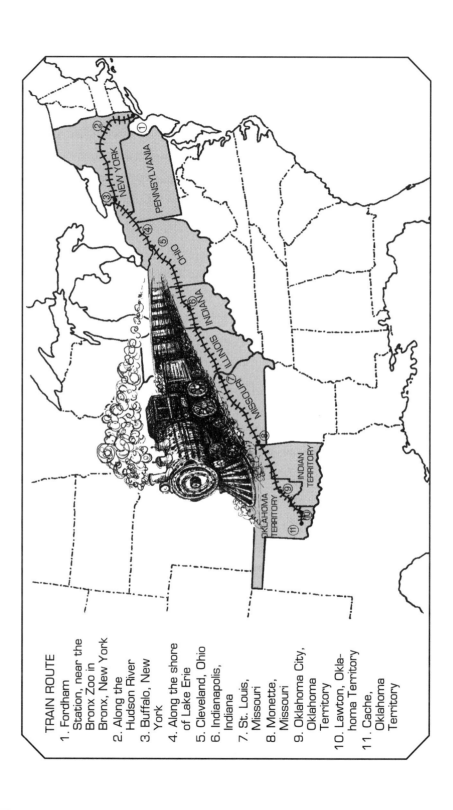

TRAIN ROUTE
1. Fordham Station, near the Bronx Zoo in Bronx, New York
2. Along the Hudson River
3. Buffalo, New York
4. Along the shore of Lake Erie
5. Cleveland, Ohio
6. Indianapolis, Indiana
7. St. Louis, Missouri
8. Monette, Missouri
9. Oklahoma City, Oklahoma Territory
10. Lawton, Oklahoma Territory
11. Cache, Oklahoma Territory

seven-eighths of an inch of an American bison," wrote Sanborn. "He resented it...."

As soon as Sanborn fell asleep, the buffalo jolted him awake. Sanborn sat up and watched. The buffalo extended his limber tongue through an opening of his crate. He decided the hay from Sanborn's bed tasted better than his own. Sanborn fell asleep again, only to be awakened by hay being tugged out from under him.

This happened several times during the night. After the seventh time, Sanborn sat straight up. He looked at his dwindling bed. If he tossed in his pillow, he calculated there was enough hay to make it until morning. With that, he resigned himself to the situation.

The following morning the men awoke several miles from the next stop—Buffalo, New York. Despite the frigid air, the three men moved around feeding and watering the buffalo. Each animal in car 6026 appeared to be traveling well. After their feast of hay, all the bison were lying down except for Comanche. The big bull refused to take advantage of his roomy crate.

Upon their arrival in Buffalo, the men entered the second car to feed and water the bison. Train inspectors

Buffalo Bits

Some folks considered Sanborn a dandy. They teased that Sanborn kept eighteen complete changes of clothing in his office. He paid a lot of attention to how he dressed and looked; yet he slept next to a buffalo with bad table manners.

•58•

approached with bad news. A steam hose from both cars had pulled free. Bolts holding one of the brake beams had also jogged loose during the night. The brake beam was almost dragging against the rails. The cars needed to be pulled for repairs.

Worse yet, the connecting train refused to take them. The men in charge said the livestock cars were not built to travel with express trains. Most manufacturers built livestock cars to move on the slower freight lines. These Arms Palace cars had been specially manufactured with air-brakes and steam connections to allow for the faster speeds.

Mitchell flew into action. He knew how train yards operated. For twenty minutes Mitchell talked with the yardmen and explained the importance of this trip. Soon the two cars were rushed to the repair tracks. Then Mitchell tackled the problem of linking to the passenger train. They could not miss their connection to Cleveland, Ohio.

Mitchell was a big bear of a man. He towered a head taller than Sanborn and Rush. Mitchell refused to back down. As far as he was concerned, arrangements had already been made. The livestock cars had the proper equipment. He talked, coaxed, and badgered. Finally, one of the officials agreed to call the Cleveland station by telephone. To everyone's relief, the traffic manager consented to the link. They would join the passenger express to Ohio.

The ride to Cleveland proved colder than the ride from New York City to Buffalo. The train rolled alongside Lake Erie. They looked out their windows and saw brown grass and leafless trees. Winter had arrived early. Stinging winds off the water entered every crack and cranny of their car. The men were not clothed in heavy robes like their traveling companions. Instead, they wrapped their overcoats around them as it began to rain.

Their car gave them feeble protection. Water penetrated every opening. A leak formed above the leftovers of Sanborn's prized hay mattress, and they discovered broken windows. The group made quick repairs. An oil-cloth was erected over the makeshift bed, and New York newspapers covered the windows. In the midst of the cold and rain, though, the largest bull uttered a cheerful sound. Comanche decided to lie down. He stretched out with a loud, contented grunt.

Despite the weather the train arrived at Cleveland, Ohio, on time. But again inspectors delivered bad news. The steam hose had fallen off somewhere along the line. The two cars must be removed for repairs. Standing in the midst of nipping cold weather, the group endured another disappointment.

At long last the yardmen repaired the steam hose. Before sunrise that Sunday morning, the train pulled out of Cleveland. Their next connection was Indianapolis, Indiana, but bad luck followed them like stuck chewing gum. At Indianapolis, inspectors again delayed the cars. Broken steam hose connections were the culprit. Finally, at ten o'clock Sunday night, the livestock cars were connected to an express train bound for St. Louis.

The hand of winter still showed its grip. As Rush, Sanborn, and Mitchell crossed over the Mississippi River, they saw frost sparkling on the bridge. Two-thirds of the adventure was nearly complete. St. Louis was the gateway to the West. The buffalo were almost home.

But delays along the way now cost them. Their planned connection to Oklahoma Territory had been missed. Railroad officials explained the Frisco Lines could only take one car at a time to Oklahoma. Steam engines handled only so much weight, and the amount of passenger travel from St. Louis was staggering. Business boomed in this midwestern hub. Travelers stood in long lines before the ticket windows and filled the waiting room. The Frisco agreed to take one livestock car that evening. The second car would travel the following night.

Mitchell tried to repair the situation. He called the Wells-Fargo superintendent and asked for his help. Together he and Mitchell approached the Frisco's general manager. The answer remained the same. The cars would have to travel separately. Eight Frisco passenger engines had collided over the past few weeks, causing a severe shortage. The general manager had no other choice. Frisco's heavy passenger traffic demanded his immediate attention.

The three quickly devised an alternative plan. Rush would travel with the first car; Sanborn and Mitchell with the second. While waiting, they fed and watered the buffalo. The animals appeared to be handling the trip well. They ate and drank as if they were already home on the plains.

Buffalo Bits

A buffalo's tongue and lips are bluish purple.

CHAPTER 7

Arrival Day

Superintendent Mattoon waited for news from Rush. Each day he rode his horse to Cache and stopped at the telegraph office. On Friday, October 11, Mattoon received a telegram. Rush sent word that he and the bison had left New York on Thursday.

News of the telegram's message spread quickly through Cache, Lawton, and the surrounding area. People guessed that if the train left New York City on Thursday, it might arrive on Sunday. Lawton lay just seventeen miles east of Cache on the railroad tracks. The buffalo train would pass through Lawton on its way to the depot in Cache.

Crowds began to gather around the Lawton depot that weekend. They could not wait to catch a glimpse of the bison. Everyone, however, was unaware of the broken steam hoses, missed connections, and other troubles that had delayed the train. They were also not aware that the telegram was wrong. The buffalo left Fordham Station late Friday night—not Thursday.

Mattoon rode into town on Sunday expecting to hear something about the bison. No telegram had arrived. He returned to Cache the next day, hoping again for some word from Rush. Mattoon waited until mid-afternoon and then rode back to the preserve. Later that evening, he returned to Cache for news of the buffalo train.

One of the Lawton newspapers reported on Monday that the train was in Oklahoma City. The *Daily News-Republican* wrote, "Large crowds of people both yesterday afternoon and today were disappointed by the failure of the herd of buffalo to arrive. Word received this afternoon states that they arrived last evening in Oklahoma City and were held over there for the state fair, which is now in progress at that place."

The news account was wrong. On Monday, October 14, Rush was still in St. Louis, Missouri. At 8:41 that Monday night, Rush said good-bye to his traveling companions. If all went as planned, he should arrive two days later in Cache, Oklahoma Territory. It would be a lonely trip, but the end was in sight.

The rest of the journey presented no further mechanical problems for Rush. Steam hoses remained in place, but trouble brewed inside car 6026. Comanche was becoming restless. He had been on this train car for four days—in a box. Being jerked and buffeted made matters worse. When Rush gave him water after leaving St. Louis, Comanche threw his head with a ferocious swing. The force hurled one horn through the wooden plank of his crate. Then with a jerk, he ripped the timber out of its place. The bison's mighty strength made front page news: "Comanche, the Big Bull and Leader of the Herd," objected strenuously to the idea of being crated.

The train arrived at the Oklahoma City depot close to midnight on Tuesday. Despite the late hour, excited throngs of people waited at the station to see the bison. It had been more than thirty years since the animal's disappearance from the southern plains. Most had never seen a buffalo. They had only heard stories from the old-timers who told how the buffalo once spread across the plains like an endless bolt of brown cloth.

Newspapers west of St. Louis carried stories of the traveling bison and Frank Rush, the "cowpuncher." Rush stepped out of car 6026 a celebrity. The gamekeeper, though, proved more than willing to show off his cargo. He wanted to spur interest in the Wichita Game Preserve and to tell people how they were saving the American bison from extinction.

Inside the livestock car were Comanche, two other bulls, three cows, and "Lottie," the six-month-old calf. Lottie was now so tame she would allow Rush to pet her. The bison in the metal cage gave people an extraordinary view. They could clearly see the mighty beast with horns atop a massive head. They marveled at the thick hair and heavy hooves. Curious onlookers also peered inside the crates. Ordinary shipments of hardware, flour, lumber, and other goods arrived daily by train, but here was a cargo of live buffalo. The massive beasts had been crated up and padded like a shipment of precious china.

The same Tuesday the bison arrived in Oklahoma City, Mattoon received a telegram from Rush. It read that one livestock car would arrive in Cache at three o'clock Wednesday afternoon. Word spread like grass fire. The buffalo were coming!

Mattoon told the horse and wagon drivers to ready their teams. Tomorrow they would transport the buffalo from Cache to the Wichita National Forest and Game Preserve.

Also on Tuesday, Sanborn and Mitchell were steaming down the tracks toward Indian Territory. The two men departed Tuesday night at 8:41—the same hour and minute Rush had left the night before. The first livestock car carried seven buffalo; theirs contained eight. No space remained for the men to lie down and sleep. They took their blankets to the express car. They created makeshift beds among the mail and other packages for delivery. Exhausted, they slept on the floor all night.

At seven o'clock the following morning, the train pulled into Monett, Missouri. Just across the state line lay Indian Territory. Sanborn and Mitchell awoke and hustled to their chores. The buffalo were waiting for their food and water. When they stepped out of the express car, a crowd of eager spectators surprised them. People wanted to see the bison.

The two zoo employees threw open the side doors. Children, men, and women pushed closer to peer inside. Many climbed inside to stand near the crates to catch a glimpse of the famous animals.

All along the way, at every stop, Sanborn and Mitchell welcomed spectators. At times people jammed the cars so thickly the air felt stale and hot. Sanborn thought he would suffocate. Individuals became so curious and excited they would not leave. Bodies pressed against the crates even as the conductor

Entrance on Cache Road. W. R. Mattoon standing in passway. Photo by Frank Rush.
(Courtesy Wichita Mountains Wildlife Refuge,
Indiahoma, Oklahoma)

yelled, "all aboard," and the wheels began to turn. The train was under way, but some people stood staring in wonder. As the train picked up speed, they finally jumped off to return home.

After sleeping all night in the express car, Sanborn and Mitchell decided to ride with the buffalo until Oklahoma City. As they traveled farther south the cold weather gave way to a warm, golden autumn. They rode with the doors open and watched the view.

"Gradually the hills gave way to low swells," wrote Sanborn, "Fields of corn, some standing, others stacked, with an occasional field of cotton, lay on every side basking in the mellow light of the early fall."

Daylight melted away, and before midnight the train pulled into Oklahoma City. Slowly the cars steamed to a stop. Out stepped Mitchell and Sanborn. It was like the arrival of royalty. People crowded around the car cheering and clapping.

Sanborn told a reporter for *The Daily Oklahoman* he was glad to be in Oklahoma City. "We have been on the road since last Friday, and have been bumped and jerked and hauled about until I am glad that the trip is just about ended," explained Sanborn. "When we left New York City we had some winter weather. It was cold and blowing a gale ... It feels good to get down here, I tell you."

Meanwhile, Rush had arrived as promised. His train pulled into Lawton on Wednesday, October 16. People had been crowding around the depot for the past four days. The delay may have disappointed them, but it did not dampen their enthusiasm. Rush talked about Comanche throwing one horn through his crate. And he proudly showed how tame little Lottie had become. The stop was not long, though.

Soon the train's wheels turned in a slow revolution and the livestock door was shut. The final destination lay seventeen miles down the tracks.

Like Lawton, the depot at Cache overflowed with cowboys, settlers, ranchers, and Indians. Comanche women arrived wrapped in bright Pendleton blankets. Some carried their babies in decorative cradleboards strapped to their backs. Young white girls and their mothers stood waiting in their best bonnets and hats. Their long skirts brushed the ground. Comanche Chief Quanah Parker arrived by wagon. Thirty-three years earlier he had attacked buffalo hunters at Adobe Walls. He had fought against the destruction of the bison. Now he waited to welcome the revered animals home.

The train steamed into the station at 3:15 P.M. Rush threw open the side doors, and people gathered around. It had worked. The gift from the New York Zoological Society had arrived safely on their doorstep.

Elder Comanche men watched as the crates were unloaded. They peered inside. Like Quanah Parker, they had not seen the "Great Spirit's Cattle" for three decades. Tears flowed down leathery faces. As boys and young men gathered around them, old warriors recalled when they and the buffalo had once roamed freely. They told of their buffalo hunts—the chase and the dust, the thrill and the danger. The hides, horns,

Buffalo Bits

Quanah Parker saw the return of the buffalo to the Wichita National Forest and Game Preserve three and a half years before his death in February 1911.

hooves, and meat of this magnificent animal had once provided everything the Indians needed to survive. Their vivid memories swirled and mixed with the crowd's excitement.

Workers placed each crated bison upon a single flatbed drawn by a team of horses. A length of rope secured the individual boxes to the wagons. By early evening they were ready. Drivers climbed atop the crates and let their legs dangle off the edges. With a snap of the reins, they started the caravan down a sandy road toward the preserve.

Twilight gathered around them as the sun dipped below the western horizon. A glowing disk of moon rose in the opposite sky lighting their twelve mile ride to the buffalo pens.

The wagons rolled at a slow but steady pace. They passed farms and crossed through valleys. As they scanned ahead, they viewed open prairie ending abruptly at dark clumps of trees. Smells of horse, grass, and buffalo surrounded them.

Several hours later the drivers heard water. They had reached the creek which flowed near the preserve's headquarters. The caravan wound its way through oak trees and then out in the open toward the buffalo pens.

There Rush met another group of Comanche who were camped at the enclosures. Entire families had been waiting several days to greet their old friends. Rush decided to leave the animals in their crates for the night. They would remain secured on the wagons.

It was near midnight and it had been a long, grueling five days for Rush, even for a man accustomed to a rough, hard life. By sunrise he was back at the buffalo pens to release the animals.

Buffalo are crated and ready for the trip to the refuge.
(Courtesy Wichita Mountains Wildlife Refuge,
Indiahoma, Oklahoma)

Every precaution had been taken to protect the bison from the dreaded Texas fever tick. Transporting the bison through the preserve by wagon kept the animals from walking through the tick-infested area. Now they were to be released into temporary holding pens until they developed an immunity to the fever. The ground was black from recent fires. Just five days earlier a crew had once again burned off any remaining grass.

One at a time, the wagons drove through two deep wedges dug out of the sod. The teams pulled their cargo through the ruts until the back end of the wagon touched the ground. Each buffalo stepped easily from its crate. Before release, all were sprayed with crude oil. Comanche, Lottie, Gypsy, and all the others moved into their corrals covered in the slick substance. The oil would prevent any ticks from biting into their skins. After the seven bison were treated, the empty wagons returned to Cache to wait for the remaining eight.

Sanborn and Mitchell arrived Thursday evening. They had been delayed in both Oklahoma City and Lawton. Seven days had passed since the two had slept in real beds with sheets and goose-down pillows. All agreed to wait until morning to transfer the bison to the preserve.

The following morning it appeared to Sanborn that the entire town of Cache had turned out to greet the buffalo. The crowds were thick and the Comanche came dressed "in their gayest clothes." By late morning the animals were loaded and ready to roll. Anxious for freedom, a young bull tapped his horns in a rhythmic beat against his crate.

The beauty of the Wichita Game Preserve captured Sanborn. "The country is certainly one of the

Crowds of onlookers view buffalo in their new home.
(Courtesy Wichita Mountains Wildlife Refuge,
Indiahoma, Oklahoma)

fairest the sun ever shone upon," he wrote. " . . . The silence was profound. It was a bit of nature as wild and free as though just created."

Rush sprayed the bison with crude oil upon arrival. Each buffalo stiffly entered the corral and hungrily ate the alfalfa. All fifteen had arrived safely. Only the bison which traveled in the wire cage suffered an injury. It was nursing a swollen leg from kicking the metal bands. The leg, however, would heal in a few days.

Mitchell wrote his uncle Hornaday that the bison had arrived safely in Oklahoma Territory. Two days later, Mitchell boarded the train to return to New York City. He was needed to supervise the Zoological Park in Hornaday's absence. Sanborn stayed two more weeks. The preserve offered a striking difference from the crowded city streets and bustling shops. He rode horseback and climbed Elk Mountain. He photographed the landscape and met local residents.

From them, no doubt, Sanborn learned of buried treasure and hidden loot. The Wichita Mountains possessed a rich heritage. Spanish explorers were known to have traveled through the area. On a cave wall were paintings of two crosses and the sign of either a turtle or sun. These messages, according to residents, pointed to buried treasure. The James gang, a band of outlaws who robbed banks and trains, were rumored to have hidden two million dollars in the Wichita Mountains.

Sanborn also heard stories of bears, wolves, and panthers. And, although he and Rush saw some signs of wolves and coyotes, he chuckled at these elaborate stories. Sanborn noted that if the wild predators were as abundant as these gentlemen portrayed, the calves did not have a chance of survival.

On October 30, Rush took Sanborn to Cache to catch the train to New York. The two men, who had traveled together through freezing temperatures and broken brake beams, said their good-byes. Sanborn should have stayed another day; he would miss an exciting event.

CHAPTER 8

Birth of a Buffalo Herd

Each day Rush worked, he made an entry in his Service Report. He could always summarize the day's events into one sentence. Two days after Sanborn and Mitchell arrived, October 19, he wrote, "Worked at the Buffalo yards feeding and watering and other general work." On October 24, he scrawled, "Fed the buffalo and rode around the Park fence with Mr. Sanborn of the New York Zoological Park."

On the day he took Sanborn to catch the train home, Rush wrote three sentences in his Service Report. The first sentence stated he fed the buffaloes and took Sanborn to Cache. The second and third entries read, "First buffalo calf born Oct. 30, 1907. Bull calf." Three sentences! Frank Rush had recorded an exciting day.

Lawton's *Daily News-Republican* gave the birth front-page coverage: " ... there is great rejoicing over the arrival of their first born back in their native

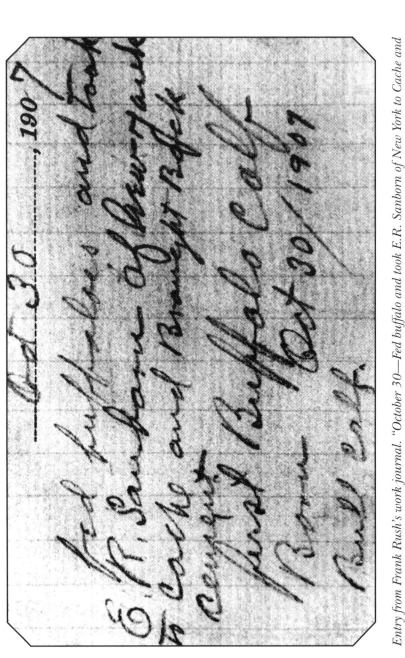

Entry from Frank Rush's work journal. "October 30—Fed buffalo and took E. R. Sanborn of New York to Cache and brought back cement. First buffalo calf born October 30/1907. Bull Calf."

(Courtesy Wichita Mountains Wildlife Refuge, Indiahoma, Oklahoma)

prairie home. It is a bull calf, born on October 30, and he is very active and comes provided with a shaggy winter suit."

Rush named the bull calf in honor of William T. Hornaday. Since creating the bison display at the National Museum, Hornaday had worked hard to protect the American bison from extinction. He began by writing a historical account. He told the nation that in fifteen years, between 1871 and 1883, millions of bison had been slaughtered by professional hunters. By 1889 less than 600 of these majestic animals existed in the United States. Others, including President Theodore Roosevelt, involved themselves in protecting the species, but Hornaday was the driving force.

The birth showed that the herd was healthy and progressing. It had only been two weeks since the animals had arrived by train. The threat of Texas fever still hung in the air. It remained Rush's main concern, and he kept a close eye on the herd. The day after Hornaday's birth, the bison were sprayed for a second time with crude oil.

Other items appeared in the newspaper besides reports about the new bull calf. Oklahoma Territory and Indian Territory were hoping to join together to form the forty-sixth state of the Union.

Buffalo Bits

Buffalo cows carry their young for approximately nine months. Lize, the cow that gave birth to Hornaday, was very pregnant during her train trip to the Game Preserve.

The vote for statehood was taken on September 17, 1907, a month before the buffalo left New York City. Now the bison were settled in their new home, and the anticipation of Oklahoma becoming the forty-sixth state made front-page news. Everyone waited to see if President Roosevelt would act on the people's vote and proclaim statehood. During his trip to Oklahoma Territory in 1905 to hunt wolves, Roosevelt had promised his support.

Two months later, though, Roosevelt had still not signed the proclamation. Everyone waited as the seasons began to change from autumn to winter. Thanksgiving was around the corner, and a golden hue settled over the preserve. Rush continued his daily visits to the buffalo corrals. His main responsibility centered on the care and feeding of the bison.

On Friday morning November 15, Rush found a surprise waiting for him. Standing next to Gypsy was a female calf that had been born sometime before dawn. The calf appeared healthy and was as big as Hornaday, the bull calf born two weeks earlier. Rush wrote five sentences in his service report that day: "Fed buffaloes [and] went to Mr. Halloways after milk cow. Worked on tower for storage tank. Earl Bentley brought alfalfa. Buffalo calf (heifer) born. Named Oklahoma."

Rush named the calf Oklahoma in honor of statehood. Coincidentally, the following day, November 16, 1907, at 10:16 in the morning, President Roosevelt signed the statehood proclamation. Oklahoma became the forty-sixth state of the Union. News of statehood was telegraphed to Guthrie, the territorial capital.

As news traveled about statehood, news traveled as well about the new birth. The *Daily News-Republican* carried the story on page one. The title read,

"Oklahoma, Second Calf to Arrive in Buffalo Camp, Comes on Statehood Day." The *Lawton Constitution-Democrat* also had a story: "Buffalo Calf Oklahoma Born on Statehood Day in National Buffalo Park. Herd Increasing Rapidly."

For years afterwards people believed the calf named Oklahoma was born on statehood day. But perhaps the newly born Oklahoma was just like the Sooners who could not wait to settle the territory. Before each land run, some homesteaders slipped unnoticed into the settlement area before the legal opening. These people were called "Sooners." Then, when the land run began, the Sooners would come out of hiding and stake their claim. Oklahoma is called the Sooner State, and the birth of the new heifer calf, Oklahoma, showed a true Sooner spirit. She sneaked in a day early.

Despite the error, the birth of a new heifer remained an important story. With just a few hundred buffalo alive in the United States, every new birth was cause for rejoicing. The birth of little Oklahoma symbolized not only the promise of a new state, but the promise of a new buffalo herd.

Buffalo Bits

Calves, when born, weigh between thirty to seventy pounds. Seventy pounds is the weight of a five- to eight-year-old human child.

Epilogue

Rush worked hard to increase the herd and to protect them from the Texas fever tick. In October 1908 he lost both Geronimo and Dolly's Mother to the fever, but he also celebrated the birth of three more calves.

Four years later, in the winter of 1912, Sanborn returned to visit Rush and the Wichita Game Preserve. Sanborn found that Comanche was still the leader, even though the herd had grown to thirty-eight members. Black Dog, the six-month-old bull calf that had traveled on the train, had grown "into a monstrous bull with a huge head and a great, shaggy mane."

Today the preserve is called the Wichita Mountains Wildlife Refuge. Elk, deer, Texas longhorn cattle, prairie dogs, and numerous other animal species share the park. The refuge maintains a buffalo herd of around 525 animals. It donates bison to other refuges and parks. In 1997 the refuge donated ten bull calves and ten heifer calves to the Lower Brule Sioux in South Dakota.

The National Bison Association reports that over 200,000 bison live in the United States, including Alaska. Most are privately owned, but many states have herds for the public to see.

Buffalo in small pasture north of buffalo yards. Photo by Frank Rush.
(Courtesy Wichita Mountains Wildlife Refuge,
Indiahoma, Oklahoma)

Glossary

bull—a male buffalo.

clavicle bones—the shoulder blades.

conservation—protecting and managing natural resources such as land, water, and animals.

corral—a pen for enclosing large animals such as horses or cattle.

cow—a female buffalo.

heifer—a young female buffalo.

homesteader—an individual who acquires title to acreage by agreeing to develop and live on the land for a specified number of years.

mining claim—the property owner has rights to minerals, such as gold, silver, or platinum, discovered and taken from his or her property.

pelage—the coat of a mammal.

poacher—an individual who hunts or fishes illegally.

tanned hides—clean, hairless animals skins which have been worked into leather.

taxidermist—an individual who prepares and mounts animal skins to create a lifelike form.

telegram—a message created by a telegraph. A telegraph is a machine that transmits and receives Morse code over a wire.

tendons—tissue that connects muscle to the skeleton.

territory—an area controlled by the United States but does not have full rights to govern itself like a state.

Texas Panhandle—the narrow strip of land in the north of Texas that is bordered by Oklahoma to the east and north.

zoological park—a zoo.

Want to Read More?

Buffalo/Bison Non-Fiction Titles:

Baker, Olaf. *Where the Buffalo Begin*. Illustrated by Stephen Gammell. Viking Children's Press, 1989.

Berman, Ruth. *American Bison*. Photographs by Cheryl Walsh Bellville. Carolrhoda Books, 1992.

Freedman, Russell. *Buffalo Hunt*. Holiday House, 1988.

Hoyt-Goldsmith, Diane. *Buffalo Days*. Photographs by Lawrence Migdale. Holiday House, 1997.

Stone, Lynn M. *Back From the Edge: The American Bison*. Rourke Corp., 1991.

Swanson, Diane. *Buffalo Sunrise: The Story of the North American Giant*. Sierra Club Books for Children, 1996.

Buffalo Fiction Titles:

Esbensen, Barbara. *The Great Buffalo Race: How the Buffalo Got its Hump; a Seneca Tale*. Illustrated by H.K. Davie. Little, Brown & Co., 1994.

Goble, Paul. *Buffalo Woman*. Macmillian, 1984.

Goble, Paul. *Iktomi and the Buffalo Skull*. Orchard Books, 1991.

Goble, Paul. *Return of the Buffalo*. National Geographic Society, 1996.

Griffis, Molly Levite. *The Buffalo in the Mall*. Illustrated by Kim Doner. Eakin Press, 1996.

Kershen, L. Michael. *Why Buffalo Roam*. Illustrated by Monica Hansen. Stemmer House, 1993.

Wallace, Bill. *Buffalo Gal*. Holiday House, 1992.

Bibliography

Books:

Bridges, William. *Gathering of Animals: An Unconventional History of the New York Zoological Society.* New York, NY: Harper & Row, Publishers, 1974.

Dary, David A. *The Buffalo Book: The Full Saga of the American Animal.* Athens, OH: Swallow Press, Ohio University Press, 1974, 1989.

Editors of Time-Life Books. *The Buffalo Hunters.* Alexandria, Virginia: Time Life Books, 1993.

Forbes, John Ripley. *In the Steps of the Great American Zoologist, William Temple Hornaday.* Illustrated by Kathleen Elgin. New York, NY: M. Evans and Company, 1966.

Garretson, Martin S. *The American Bison: The Story of its Extermination as a Wild Species and its Restoration Under Federal Protection.* New York, NY: New York Zoological Society, 1938.

Garretson, Martin S. *A Short History of the American Bison: Distribution, Habits, Trails, Extermination, Etc., For Use in Schools.* New York, NY: The American Bison Society, 1934.

Haley, J. Evetts. *Fort Concho and the Texas Frontier.* San Angelo, TX: San Angelo Standard-Times, 1952.

Haley, James L. *The Buffalo War: The History of the Red River Indian Uprising of 1874.* Garden City, NJ: Doubleday, 1976.

Halloran, Art. *The Nature Man's Stories of the Wichita Mountains.* Lawton, OK: Art Halloran, 1972.

Hamilton, W. T. *My Sixty Years on the Plains Trapping, Trading and Indian Fighting.* New York, NY: Forest and Stream Publishing Co., 1905.

Hornaday, William T. *Thirty Years War for Wild Life*. Reprint edition, [nc]: Arno Press, 1970.

Jackson, Clyde L. and Grace Jackson. *Quanah Parker, Last Chief of the Comanches: A Study in Southwestern Frontier History*. New York, NY: Exposition Press, 1963.

Marrin, Albert. *Plains Warrior: Chief Quanah Parker and the Comanches*. New York, NY: Atheneum Books for Young Readers, 1996.

Morgan, E. Buford. *The Wichita Mountains: An Ancient Oasis of the Prairies*. Waco, TX: Texlan Press, 1973.

Nye, Colonel W. S. *Carbine and Lance: The Story of Old Fort Sill*. Norman, OK: University of Oklahoma Press, 1943.

Ramsay, Jack C., Jr. *Sunshine on the Prairie: The Story of Cynthia Ann Parker*. Austin, TX: Eakin Press, 1990.

Trefethen, James B. *Crusade for Wildlife: Highlights in Conservation Progress*. Harrisburg, PA: The Stackpole Company, and New York, NY: Boone and Crockett Club, 1961.

Webb, Walter Prescott. *The Great Plains*. Boston, MA: Ginn and Company, 1931.

Correspondence:

Letter from H. R. Mitchell (Cache, Oklahoma) to W. T. Hornaday (New York City, New York) on October 19, 1907. Library, Wildlife Conservation Society, Bronx, New York.

Journals:

Brill, Charles J. "What Indian Tongues Could Tell: Introducing Frank Rush." *Southwest Wilds & Waters, A National Outdoor Magazine for the Great Southwest*, Vol. II, No. 4, April 1930, pp. 15-17 & 42.

Haley, Jack D. "The Wichita Mountains: The Struggle to Preserve a Wilderness, Part I." *Great Plains Journal*, Fall 1973, pp. 71-99.

Haley, Jack D. "The Wichita Mountains: The Struggle to Preserve a Wilderness, Part II." *Great Plains Journal*, Spring 1974, pp. 149-186.

Halloran, Arthur F. "50 Years Ago This Fall The Bison Returned to the Plains," *Animal Kingdom: Magazine of the New York Zoological Society*, IX (Sept-Oct, 1957), pp. 130-134.

Rister, C. C. "The Significance of the Destruction of the Buffalo in the Southwest," *Southwestern Historical Quarterly*, Vol. XXXIII, No. 1, July 1929, pp. 34-49.

Sanborn, Elwin R. "The National Bison Herd: An Account of the Transportation of the Bison from the Zoological Park to the Wichita Range." *Zoological Society Bulletin*, Vol. II, Nos. 24-60, October 1906–November 1913. New York, NY: New York Zoological Society, 1915.

Sanborn, Elwin R. "An Object Lesson in Bison Preservation: The Wichita National Bison Herd After Five Years." *Zoological Society Bulletin*, May 1913, pp. 990-993.

Strickland, Rex, editor. "The Recollections of W. S. Glenn, Buffalo Hunter," *Panhandle-Plains Historical Review*, Vol. XXII, 1949

Newspapers:

The Daily-News Republican, 1907 (Lawton, Oklahoma)

The Daily Oklahoman, Sunday, October 20, 1907, p. 4

Kansas City Star, October 1907

The Kansas City Star, Sunday, May 28, 1911, 10A

Oklahoma Farm News & Mineral Kingdom, December 28, 1905, p. 6

The Sunday Oklahoman, November 15, 1964, p. 20A

The Lawton Constitution, October 11, 1906, p. 6

Lawton Constitution-Democrat, (1907)

The New York Times, October 11, 1907, p. 14

The New York Times, December 4, 1965, p. L33

Annual Reports:

Bard, Frederic S., compiler. *Outdoor Oklahoma: The 1914 Annual Report of the State Game and Fish Warden, John B. Doolin, to the Governor of the State of Oklahoma, The Honorable Lee Cruce*, p. 26-31.

Hornaday, William T. "The Extermination of the American Bison with a Sketch of its Discovery and Life History." *The Annual Report of the Board of Regents of the Smithsonian Institution Showing the Operations, Expenditures, and Condition of the Institution for the Year Ending June 30, 1887, Part II*. Washington: Government Printing Office, 1889, p. 367-548.

Hornaday, William T. "The Founding of the Wichita National Bison Herd." *Annual Report of the American Bison Society, 1905-1907*. [New York, NY]: American Bison Society, 1908, p. 54-69.

Loring, J. Alden. "The Wichita Buffalo Range: A Report to the New York Zoological Society as an Inspection of the Wichita Forest and Game Reserve in Oklahoma, to Select a Suitable

Location for a Buffalo Range." *Tenth Annual Report of the New York Zoological Society, 1905.* New York, NY: Office of the Society, January 1906.

Pamphlet:

Forest Service. "The Wichita National Forest and Game Preserve." Miscellaneous Circular No. 36, United States Department of Agriculture, Washington, D.C., Issued May 1925. Revised June 1928.

Thesis:

Haley, Jack Dan. "A History of the Establishment of the Wichita National Forest and Game Preserve, 1901-1908." University of Oklahoma, 1973.

Other Sources:

Cook, Bird I., Guard, Service Report, November 1907. Wichita Mountains Wildlife Refuge Headquarters, Oklahoma.

Collinson, Frank. "Jack Bickerdyke—Buffalo Hunter and Scout. (Paper) [n.d.] Panhandle-Plains Museum, Research Center, Canyon, Texas.

Hamner, Laura V. "Buffalo Days and Buffalo Ways," [n.d.] Works Projects Administration. Panhandle-Plains Museum, Research Center, Canyon, Texas.

Mattoon, W. R., Acting Supervisor, Service Report of September—November 1907. Wichita Mountains Wildlife Refuge Headquarters, Oklahoma.

Mooar, J. Wright to J. Evetts Haley, November 25, 1927. (Interview) Panhandle-Plains Museum, Research Center, Canyon, Texas.

Mooar, J. Wright to F.P.H., J. B. Slaughter Jr., Jim Weatherford, May 15, 1936. (Interview) Panhandle-Plains Museum, Research Center, Canyon, Texas.

Reighard, George W. as told to A. B. MacDonald. "What an Old Buffalo Hunter Saw Who Helped to Exterminate the Herds that Darkened the Plains." (Attributed to the *Kansas City Star*, November 30, 1930.) Kansas State Historical Society, Wichita, Kansas.

Rush, Frank, Forest Guard, Service Report of September—November 1907. Wichita Mountains Wildlife Refuge Headquarters, Oklahoma.

Index